Linux

Linux For Beginners

Your Step By Step Guide Of Becoming A Linux Command Line Ninja

PS: I Owe You!

Thank you for stopping by.

My name is Antony and I am passionate about teaching people literally everything I know about different aspects of life. I am an author and a ghostwriter. I run a small ghostwriting company with slightly over 100 writers. My wife (Faith) and I manage the business along with several other members of the team (editors).

Nice to meet you!

I started publishing (at Fantonpublishers.com) because I'd love to impart the knowledge I gather every single day in my line of work (reading and editing over 10 ghostwritten books every single day). My ghostwriting company deals with literally every topic under the sun, which puts me at a very unique position to learn more in a month than I learnt in my 4 years as a Bachelor of Commerce, Accounting, student. I am constantly answering questions from my friends, relatives and even strangers on various topics that I come across every day at work.

After several years of helping people to achieve different goals (e.g. weight loss, making money online, human resources, management, investing, stress reduction, depression, budgeting, saving etc.) offline thanks to my 'street' as well as 'class' knowledge on different topics, I realized I could be of better help to the world by publishing what I learn. My books are a reflection of what I have been gathering over the years. That's why they are not just focused on one niche but every niche possible out there.

If you would love to be part of my lovely audience who want to change multiple aspects of their life, subscribe to our newsletter http://bit.ly/2fantonpubnewbooks or follow us on social media to receive notifications whenever we publish new books on any niche. You can also send me an email; I would love to hear from you!

PS: Valuable content is my bread and butter. And since I have lots of it to go around, I can share it freely (not everything is about money - **changing lives comes first!**)

I promise; I am busy just as you are and won't spam (I hate spam too)!

Antony,

Website: http://www.fantonpublishers.com/

Email: Support@fantonpublishers.com

Twitter: https://twitter.com/FantonPublisher

Facebook Page:
https://www.facebook.com/Fantonpublisher/

Private Facebook Group For Readers:
https://www.facebook.com/groups/FantonPublishers/

Pinterest: https://www.pinterest.com/fantonpublisher/

Some of the best things in life are free, right?

As a sign of good faith, I will start by giving out content that will help you to implement not only everything I teach in this book but in every other book I write. The content is about life transformation, presented in bit size pieces for easy implementation. I believe that without such a checklist, you are likely to have a hard time implementing anything in this book and any other thing you set out to do religiously and sticking to it for the long haul. It doesn't matter whether your goals relate to weight loss, relationships, personal finance, investing, personal development, improving communication in your family, your overall health, finances, improving your sex life, resolving issues in your relationship, fighting PMS successfully, investing, running a successful business, traveling etc. With a checklist like the one I will show you, you can bet that anything you do will seem a lot easier to implement until the end. This checklist will help you to start well and not lose steam along the way, until the very end. Therefore, even if you don't continue reading this book, at least read the one thing that will help you in every other aspect of your life.

Send me a message on support@fantonpublishers.com and I will send you my 5 Pillar Life Transformation Checklist.

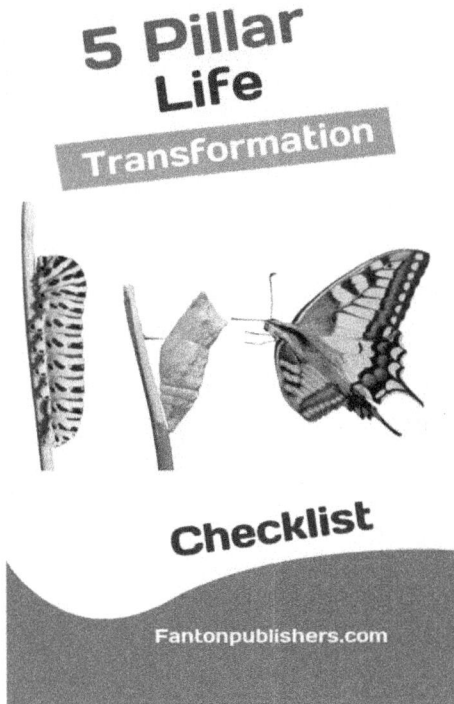

Your life will never be the same again (if you implement what's in this book), I promise.

Introduction

For some time now, there has been a rising misconception that Linux is harder to use than other operating systems, with some vendors even suggesting that the OS is only suitable for users only with an interest for open source programming.

If you've encountered any problems working with Linux, and have come here to try and learn the software, there's one thing you have to understand first. This operating system is not the problem. The only issue is that it's different; different from the other operating systems you've perhaps used your entire life- just like north Americans learn to drive on the right side of the road and the UK and elsewhere, learn to drive on the left.

With this guide, I will dispel the notion that working with Linux is hard by teaching you step by step everything you need to learn about this OS, particularly the use of the command line, and also how to use that knowledge to become a master of Linux

You'll see that not only is Linux easy to use, it's also the best OS we have today.

So, if you've been desiring to understand how to use Linux and take advantage of the many opportunities that the knowledge offers, this is your guide. It will help you understand everything you need to know about Linux- right from the basics, making the requisite installations to the terminal and many other important skills.

Table of Contents

PS: I Owe You!...2

Introduction 6

An Comprehensive Introduction To Linux............. 12

A Little Background 12

Essential Parts Of A Linux System 14

Choosing Your Distribution (Distro) 16

How To Download And Install Tiny Core Linux 18

Prepare For Installation...................................22

The File Type..24

Opening The Terminal 27

Working With The Shell (Terminal) 28

The Basic Commands..28

Pwd 28

Is..28

Cd 29

Rmdir and mkdir 30

Rm 30

Touch.. 31

Man & --help 31

Cp 32

Mv 32

Locate 33

The Intermediate Commands 33

Echo 33

Cat 34

Nano, jed, vi 34

Df 36

Tar 36

Zip and unzip 37

Uname 37

Apt-get 37

Chmod 38

Hostname 39

Ping 39

How To Create Basic Scripts 41

Your First Shell Script 41

Having Arguments In A Re-Usable Shell Script . 43

Bash "If Statements" 46

   Basic "If Statements" 46

   The Test...48

   Final Word: Indenting 51

Conclusion...53

Do You Like My Book & Approach To Publishing? 54

6 Things 54

   1: First, I'd Love It If You Leave a Review of This Book on Amazon. 55

   2: Check Out My Other Books 55

   3: Let's Get In Touch...56

   4: Grab Some Freebies On Your Way Out; Giving Is Receiving, Right? 57

   5: Suggest Topics That You'd Love Me To Cover To Increase Your Knowledge Bank. 57

   6: Subscribe To My Newsletter To Know When I Publish New Books. 57

My Other Books..59

   Weight Loss Books 59

   General Weight Loss Books 59

   Weight Loss Books On Specific Diets 60

Ketogenic Diet Books 60

Intermittent Fasting Books 61

Any Other Diet.. 61

Relationships Books 61

Personal Development 62

Personal Finance & Investing Books.................. 63

Health & Fitness Books 63

Book Summaries.. 64

All The Other Niches 65

   Travel Books 65

   Dog Training.. 66

   World Issues Books 66

See You On The Other Side! 67

Stay With Me On My Journey To Making Passive Income Online 68

PSS: Let Me Also Help You Save Some Money!..... 70

An Comprehensive Introduction To Linux

A Little Background

Originally, Linux was developed merely as a hobby project by a programmer known as Linus Torvalds in the early 1990s while at the University Of Helsinki In Finland. The project was inspired by a small Unix (an operating system) system called Minix that had been developed by professor Andy Tanebaum who used the Unix code to teach students of that university about operating systems. At that time, Unix was only used in universities for academic purposes. The professor developed Minix (a little clone of Unix) to effectively teach his students about operating systems with a bit more depth.

Linus was inspired by Minix and developed his own clone, which he named Linux.

On 5th October 1991, version 0.02- which was the first version of Linux, was announced by Linus. While this version was able to run the Bourne shell (bash)- the command line interface- and a compiler called GCC, there wasn't so much else to it.

The version 0.03 was released some time later and then the version number was bumped up to 0.10, as more people began embracing the software. After a couple more revisions, Linus released version 0.95 in March 1992 as a way of reflecting his expectation that the system was prepared for an 'official' release real soon.

About one year and a half later (December 1993), the version was finally made it to 1.0.

Today, Linux is a total clone of Unix and has since been able to reach a user base spanning industries and continents. The people who understand it see and appreciate its use in virtually everything- from cars to smartphones, home appliances like fridges and supercomputers, this operating system is everywhere. Linux actually runs the largest part of the internet, the computers making all the scientific breakthroughs you're hearing about every other day and the world's stock exchanges.

As you appreciate its existence, don't forget that this operating system was (and still is) the most secure, reliable and hassle-free operating system available before it became the best platform to run servers, desktops and embedded systems all over the globe.

With that short history, I believe you are now ready for some information to get you up to speed on this marvelous platform.

Essential Parts Of A Linux System

Just like other Mac OS X and Windows 10, Linux is an operating system. It is made up of the following pieces:

The bootloader- This is the software that manages your computer's boot processes. Simply put, it is the splash screen that pops up and then disappears to boot into the operating system.

The kernel- If you've done some research into Linux before, you should have come across this word countless times. It refers to the piece of the whole that's referred to as *Linux*. It is the core of the system; it manages peripheral devices, CPU and memory.

Daemons- These are the background services such as scheduling, sound and printing that either start when you log into your computer or during the boot process.

Shell- You've probably also heard this word too many times as well or the *Linux command line,* which at one time scared many people away from Linux (perhaps because they thought they had to learn some mind-numbing command line structure to use the OS). The shell is the command process that lets you control your computer through commands by typing them into a text interface. Today, you can work with Linux without even touching the command line but it's important to work with it, as we are going to see shortly.

***Graphical server*-** This is simply the sub-system that displays graphics on your monitor. It is commonly known as x or the x server.

***The desktop environment*-** This is the actual implementation of the metaphor 'desktop' that is made of programs running on the visible surface of the operating system that you will interact with directly. You have numerous desktop environments to choose from which include gnome, enlightenment, xfce, utility and cinnamon. The desktop environment comes with a bundle of built-in applications, which include configuration tools, file managers, games and web browsers- among others.

***Applications*-** As you may already know, desktop environments don't usually offer the full array of apps. Linux provides thousands of software titles, which you can easily access and install, which is the same case with Windows and Mac.

The above descriptions will assist you sail through the rest of the book easily. Let's now get to the part where we start using the program. The first step is choosing the distribution, as you will find out next.

Choosing Your Distribution (Distro)

Before we get started with the command line, we have to make sure you are all set up. The first thing you need to do therefore is select your distribution. Unlike Windows, Linux doesn't have a single version, and that's why we have many Linux 'distributions'.

These distributions take the kernel and combine it with other software such as a desktop environment, graphical server, web browser and many more. A distribution thus unites all these elements into one operating system that you can install and work with.

From a beginner user versions to intermediate and advanced user versions, there are versions to suit any level or need. All you have to do is download your preferred version into a USB thumb drive and install it to any number of machines you like.

Which distribution should you go for?

You need a distro that is easy to install, it needs to have great applications on it and needs to be easy to use for everyday activities. Moreover, the distro needs to be easy to tweak when the need arises. It is for these reasons that I recommend the tiny core distro that weighs about 11 MB.

Introducing... tiny core!

Besides satisfying those parameters, tiny core saves so much on size and only requires you to have a wired network connection during its initial setup. The recommended amount of RAM you need here is only 128MB.

Well, you can take other considerations while choosing your distro, but it all depends on what you want to use it for. The distro we'll work with here is clearly ideal for someone who's just dipping their feet into Linux- without any considerable experience.

Also known as TCL, Tiny core Linux is a very specific distro, specially designed to be nomadic. Just like other distros, you can bring it with you and run it from a USB drive, CD or hard disk.

For this section, we're going to be using TCL as an example of how you can download and install a Linux distro.

How To Download And Install Tiny Core Linux

You can download TCL in the three different distros from this page.

http://tinycorelinux.net/downloads.html

You can take any of them and start the process. In the startup menu, you have to choose the option labelled 'core only'. Well, the core only (also known as the microcore) interface is simply a text based interface. You can just begin typing some commands here.

Let's try to download and install the TCL installation package on a hard disk.

The first command you'll use is 'tce-load —wi tc-install'. You don't have to type the 'tce' extension.

Note: In the code that follows, all the typed commands are in red, and their outputs are in black. For the first command, you'll get the following output:

```
tc@box:~$ tce-load -wi tc-install

tc-install.tcz.dep OK

fltk-1.3.tcz.dep OK

libXext.tcz.dep OK

libX11.tcz.dep OK

libxcb.tcz.dep OK

Downloading: libpng.tcz

Connecting to repo.tinycorelinux.net (89.22.99.37:80)

libpng.tcz 100% |*****************************| 94208 0:00:00 ETA

libpng.tcz: OK

Downloading: libjpeg-turbo.tcz

Connecting to repo.tinycorelinux.net (89.22.99.37:80)

libjpeg-turbo.tcz 100% |*****************************| 116k 0:00:00 ETA

libjpeg-turbo.tcz: OK

Downloading: libXdmcp.tcz

Connecting to repo.tinycorelinux.net (89.22.99.37:80)

libXdmcp.tcz 100% |*****************************| 20480 0:00:00 ETA

libXdmcp.tcz: OK

Downloading: libXau.tcz

Connecting to repo.tinycorelinux.net (89.22.99.37:80)

libXau.tcz 100% |*****************************| 12288 0:00:00 ETA

libXau.tcz: OK

Downloading: libxcb.tcz

Connecting to repo.tinycorelinux.net (89.22.99.37:80)

libxcb.tcz 100% |*****************************| 208k 0:00:00 ETA
```

libxcb.tcz: OK

Downloading: libX11.tcz

Connecting to repo.tinycorelinux.net (89.22.99.37:80)

libX11.tcz 100% |*****************************| 968k 0:00:00 ETA

libX11.tcz: OK

Downloading: libXext.tcz

Connecting to repo.tinycorelinux.net (89.22.99.37:80)

libXext.tcz 100% |*****************************| 28672 0:00:00 ETA

libXext.tcz: OK

Downloading: fltk-1.3.tcz

Connecting to repo.tinycorelinux.net (89.22.99.37:80)

fltk-1.3.tcz 100% |*****************************| 440k 0:00:00 ETA

fltk-1.3.tcz: OK

Downloading: perl5.tcz

Connecting to repo.tinycorelinux.net (89.22.99.37:80)

perl5.tcz 100% |*****************************| 12892k 0:00:00 ETA

perl5.tcz: OK

Downloading: dosfstools.tcz

Connecting to repo.tinycorelinux.net (89.22.99.37:80)

dosfstools.tcz 100% |*****************************| 57344 0:00:00 ETA

dosfstools.tcz: OK

Downloading: syslinux.tcz

Connecting to repo.tinycorelinux.net (89.22.99.37:80)

syslinux.tcz 100% |*****************************| 2284k 0:00:00 ETA

syslinux.tcz: OK

```
Downloading: tc-install.tcz

Connecting to repo.tinycorelinux.net (89.22.99.37:80)

tc-install.tcz 100% |*****************************| 20480 0:00:00 ETA

tc-install.tcz: OK

tc@box:~$
```

This process will take a few minutes, but it depends on your internet link as well.

Prepare For Installation

At this point, you are now ready to install the TCL on the hard disk. You have to run the installation script as the super user- root (oh, this means you've got full control of the operating system).

tc@box:~$ sudo tc-install.sh

The script will clear the screens in between steps. The initial screen is the core installation.

Install from [R]unning OS, from booted [C]drom, or from [I]so file.
c

Now press 'enter' to confirm your choice on each screen. We'll thus do that here. In the next screen, you have a choice for the type of installation; you can select the frugal installation (this refers to the installation on your hard disk) or removable media (USB drive) installation.

Select install type for **/mnt/sro/boot/core.gz Frugal**

* Use for frugal **hard drive** installations.

Note: You will be prompted for disk/partion and formatting options.

HDD * Use for **pendrives**. Your BIOS must support **USB-HDD** booting.
* A single FAT partition will be made.

Note: Requires dosfstools extension. **Warning:** This is a whole drive installation!

Zip * Use for **pendrives**. Drive will be formatted into two FAT partitions.
* One small one for **USB_ZIP** boot compatibility, and used to hold Tiny Core.

* The remaining partition will be used for backup & extensions. **Note:** Requires dosfstools and perl extensions.

Warning: This is a whole drive installation! **Select Install type [F]rugal, [H]DD, [Z]ip. (f/h/z): f**

The 'f' in this case stands for 'frugal' installation. You're essentially building a virtual machine that works permanently, from the hard disk.

Now that you're doing a hard drive installation, you'll receive a prompt to perform disk partitioning and formatting.

First of all, you'll choose whether you're going to use the whole disk or an existing partition. For the latter, you can enter either (1-2) or (q)uit: 1. But remember that you cannot use the 'existing partition' option if you did not make any partition before installation. In this case, go with the first option: *whole disk.*

Once you select this option, you'll see another screen with all the disks in the system where you have to select the right one. They are described as sdb, sda, sro and so forth. Sro is for cd-rom, fdo is for the floppy disk drive and sda is for the hard drive.

Select disk for core

1. fdo

2. sda

Enter selection (1 - 2) or (q)uit: 2

Your choice obviously is number 2.

The next thing is selecting whether or not you want a bootloader. If you're installing TCL on a blank disk, you will definitely need it. Since your system is empty, you have to choose yes- this is represented by 'y'.

The File Type

The next step entails selecting a file format, and your choice will depend on the type of media. If you want to install your software on a USB pen drive or something similar, you should select what is referred to a non-journaling file system such as vfat or ext2.

The ext4 and ext3 systems on the other hand have more writing cycles on the disk because they've been designed for robustness on data loss. If your USB is not designed for heavy writing operations therefore, it may malfunction. So select your file format based on your drive.

Select Formatting Option for sda

1. ext2

2. ext3

3. ext4

4. vfat

Enter selection (1 - 4) or (q)uit: 3

On the screen that follows, add the options for tce app restore directory and the display resolution:

Enter space separated boot options:

Example: vga=normal syslog showapps waitusb=5

vga=788 tce=hda1

Select 'y' on the next screen to start the installation process:

Last chance to exit before destroying all data on sda

Continue (y/..)?

When the installation process is successful, you will see something displayed on your screen that looks like this:

Writing zero's to beginning of /dev/sda

Partitioning /dev/sda

Formatting /dev/sda1

1+0 records in

1+0 records out

440 bytes (440B) copied, 0.000846 seconds, 507.9KB/s

UUID="FA02-C854"

Setting up core image on /mnt/sda1

Applying syslinux.

Installation has completed

Press Enter key to continue.

Congratulations! Your software has been installed.

Opening The Terminal

When your installation is complete, you can press either one of the following to open the terminal

- Alt+f2, and then enter gnome-terminal and tap okay or enter

- Ctrl+alt+t (Ubuntu)

- Lxterminal (Raspberry Pi)

If you had a problem cracking some elements of code in the illustrations above, the chapter below will explain to you what they mean.

Working With The Shell (Terminal)

As you already know, shell is the program that receives your commands and feeds them to the operating system to process, and then displays the output. This chapter will cover the basic commands that are used in Linux shell.

The Basic Commands

Pwd

When you first open the terminal, you'll essentially be in the user's home directory. To know which directory you're in, simply use the command 'pwd'. You will get the absolute path- that is, the path that begins from the base of the file system, also known as the root. It is essentially denoted by the forward slash '/'.

You'll thus get something like this:

/home/username

```
nayso@Alok-Aspire:~$ pwd
/home/nayso
```

Is

You can use the command 'is' when you want to know what files are in your directory (the directory you're currently in). You will be able to see all hidden files with the command 'is-a'

```
nayso@Alok-Aspire:~$ ls
Desktop          itsuserguide.desktop  reset-settings      VCD_Copy
Documents        Music                 School_Resources    Videos
Downloads        Pictures              Students_Works_10
examples.desktop Public                Templates
GplatesProject   Qgis Projects         TuxPaint-Pictures
```

Cd

You'll use this command to go to a specific directory. For instance, if you are currently in the home folder and want to access the 'downloads' folder, you can enter 'cd downloads'. Don't forget that this command is case sensitive. You also have to type in the folder name exactly as it is. Nonetheless, there is a problem with these commands. You can imagine having a folder called raspberry pi. This means that you have to type in 'cd raspberry pi' but the shell only takes the second part (argument) of the command as a different one, this therefore means that you will receive an error stating that the directory doesn't exist. In this case therefore, you should use a backward slash:

'cd raspberry\ pi'

Typing only 'cd' and pressing enter takes you to the home directory. You can type 'cd..' to go back from a folder to the previous folder you can enter 'cd..' . That means that the two dots denote *back*.

```
nayso@Alok-Aspire:~$ cd Downloads
nayso@Alok-Aspire:~/Downloads$ cd
nayso@Alok-Aspire:~$ cd Raspberry\ Pi
nayso@Alok-Aspire:~/Raspberry Pi$ cd ..
nayso@Alok-Aspire:~$ 
```

Rmdir and mkdir

When you want to create a folder or a directory, use the command 'mkdir'. For instance, if you want to create a folder named 'diy', you will type 'mkdir diy'. Don't forget that if you want to make a directory called 'diy hacking', you'll have to type 'mkdir diy\ hacking'.

On the other hand, you will use 'rmdir' when you want to delete a directory. However, you can only use rmdir to delete an empty directory; just use 'rm' if you want to delete a directory that contains files.

```
nayso@Alok-Aspire:~/Desktop$ ls
nayso@Alok-Aspire:~/Desktop$ mkdir DIY
nayso@Alok-Aspire:~/Desktop$ ls
DIY
nayso@Alok-Aspire:~/Desktop$ rmdir DIY
nayso@Alok-Aspire:~/Desktop$ ls
nayso@Alok-Aspire:~/Desktop$
```

Rm

Besides what I've mentioned above, you can use 'rm-r' to only delete the directory. The 'rm' command will delete the folder as well as the files it contains.

```
nayso@Alok-Aspire:~/Desktop$ ls
newer.py  New Folder
nayso@Alok-Aspire:~/Desktop$ rm newer.py
nayso@Alok-Aspire:~/Desktop$ ls
New Folder
nayso@Alok-Aspire:~/Desktop$ rm -r New\ Folder
nayso@Alok-Aspire:~/Desktop$ ls
nayso@Alok-Aspire:~/Desktop$
```

Touch

This command will help you make a file, which can be anything from an empty zip file to an empty txt file. For instance:

'touch new.txt'

```
nayso@Alok-Aspire:~/Desktop$ ls
nayso@Alok-Aspire:~/Desktop$ touch new.txt
nayso@Alok-Aspire:~/Desktop$ ls
new.txt
```

Man & --help

The command 'man' will assist you know more about a command, and how to use it. It shows you the command's manual pages. For instance, 'man cd' shows the 'cd' command's manual pages.

When you type in the command name, the argument will enable it show the ways through which the command can be used- for instance 'cd -help'.

```
TOUCH(1)                        User Commands                        TOUCH(1)

NAME
       touch - change file timestamps

SYNOPSIS
       touch [OPTION]... FILE...

DESCRIPTION
       Update  the   access   and modification times of each FILE to the current
       time.

       A FILE argument that does not exist is created empty, unless -c  or  -h
       is supplied.

       A  FILE  argument  string of - is handled specially and causes touch to
       change the times of the file associated with standard output.

       Mandatory arguments to long options are  mandatory  for  short  options
       too.

       -a      change only the access time

 Manual page touch(1) line 1 (press h for help or q to quit)
```

Cp

This command is used to copy files through the command line. 'cp' takes two arguments which include:

- The file's location

- Where to copy

```
nayso@Alok-Aspire:~/Desktop$ ls /home/nayso/Music/
nayso@Alok-Aspire:~/Desktop$ cp new.txt /home/nayso/Music/
nayso@Alok-Aspire:~/Desktop$ ls /home/nayso/Music/
new.txt
```

Mv

This command is used when moving commands through the command line. You can also use this command to rename a certain file. For instance, if you want the file 'text' to read 'new', you can use 'mv text new'. Just like the command 'cp', it takes the two arguments.

32

```
nayso@Alok-Aspire:~/Desktop$ ls
new.txt
nayso@Alok-Aspire:~/Desktop$ mv new.txt newer.txt
nayso@Alok-Aspire:~/Desktop$ ls
newer.txt
```

Locate

When you want to locate a file in the Linux system, you can use 'locate'. It is similar to the search command in Windows OS. You will find it useful when you don't know the file's actual name or where it is saved. You can use the '-i' argument with the command to ignore the case (this means it doesn't matter whether it's lowercase or uppercase).

Therefore, if you want a file that contains the word 'hello', you can enter 'locate –i hello' and you'll get a list of all files within your Linux system that contains that word. If you can remember two words, you can use the asterisk (*) to separate them. For instance assume you want to locate a file that contains the words 'this' and 'hello'. You'll use the command 'locate –i *this*hello'.

```
nayso@Alok-Aspire:~$ locate newer.txt
/home/nayso/Desktop/newer.txt
nayso@Alok-Aspire:~$ locate *DIY*Hacking*
/home/nayso/DIY Hacking
```

Now let's take a look at:

The Intermediate Commands

Echo

This command will help you move some data, usually in text form into a file. For instance, if you want to add to another that is already made or make a new text file altogether, all you have to do is simply enter:

'echo hello, my name is alok>> new.txt'.

Here, you don't need to use the backward slash to separate the spaces because you'll add two triangle brackets when you complete what you need to write.

Cat

This command is used to display file contents. You'll find it important when you want to view programs easily.

```
nayso@Alok-Aspire:~/Desktop$ echo hello, my name is alok >> new.txt
nayso@Alok-Aspire:~/Desktop$ cat new.txt
hello, my name is alok
nayso@Alok-Aspire:~/Desktop$ echo this is another line >> new.txt
nayso@Alok-Aspire:~/Desktop$ cat new.txt
hello, my name is alok
this is another line
```

Nano, jed, vi

First of all, the command 'nano' is a great text editor that denotes the colored keywords, besides being able to recognize most languages. Vi on the other hand is simpler than nano. You can make a new file or use the editor to modify a file. Let's take an example.

You want to make a file with the name 'check.txt'. You can use the 'nano check.txt' command to make it.

After editing, you can save the files with the sequence ctrl+x, and then y (yes) or n (no).

```
  GNU nano 2.2.6              File: check.txt

This is a file named check.txt edited in Nano Text Editor!!









Save modified buffer (ANSWERING "No" WILL DESTROY CHANGES) ?
 Y  Yes
 N  No              ^C  Cancel
```

Sudo

'sudo' means 'super user do'. That means that if you want to have any command implemented with root or administrative privileges, you can invoke the 'sudo' command.

Let's take an example:

You want to edit the file 'viz. Alsa-base.conf' or any other file that requires root permission. You can use the following command:

'sudo nano alsa-base.conf'

You can use the 'sudo bash' command to enter the root command line, and then enter your user password. Another command you can use to do this is 'su', but you'll have to set a root password before that. To do that, you can enter the 'sudo passwd' command and then enter the new password.

```
nayso@Alok-Aspire:~/Desktop$ sudo passwd
[sudo] password for nayso:
Enter new UNIX password:
Retype new UNIX password:
passwd: password updated successfully
nayso@Alok-Aspire:~/Desktop$ su
Password:
root@Alok-Aspire:/home/nayso/Desktop# █
```

Df

If you want to see how much disk space you have left in each of your system's partitions, you can use the 'df' command. All you have to do is type it in your command line and you'll be able to see each mounted partition and how much space is used or available in kilobytes. You can use the command 'df -m' if you want to see it displayed in megabytes.

```
root@Alok-Aspire:/home/nayso/Desktop# df -m
Filesystem     1M-blocks  Used  Available  Use%  Mounted on
udev                 940     1        940    1%  /dev
tmpfs                191     2        189    1%  /run
/dev/sda5          96398 23466      68013   26%  /
none                   1     0          1    0%  /sys/fs/cgroup
none                   5     0          5    0%  /run/lock
none                 951     1        950    1%  /run/shm
none                 100     1        100    1%  /run/user
```

Tar

This command is useful when you want to work with tarballs (archives or files compressed in archives) in the command line. You can use it to do so much; you can use it to compress or un-compress various kinds of tar archives such as .tar.gz,

.tar and .tar.bz2. It works based on the arguments you give it. For instance, 'tar -cvf' will create a .tar archive, -xvf will untar a tar archive and −tvf will list the archive's contents. You can take a look at <u>these</u> examples of tar commands to learn more.

Zip and unzip

You'll use 'zip' to compress files into a zip archive and 'unzip' to extract them from a zip archive.

Uname

This command helps you see information about the system your distro is running at the moment. To print out the information about the system, you can use the 'uname-a' command. You'll have the kernel release date, processor type, version and so on.

```
nayso@Alok-Aspire:~$ uname -a
Linux Alok-Aspire 4.4.0-22-generic #40~14.04.1-Ubuntu SMP Fri May 13 17:27:18 UT
C 2016 i686 i686 i686 GNU/Linux
```

Apt-get

'apt' comes in when you want to work with packages in Linux. 'apt-get' installs the packages. You'll require root privileges here so you'll have to use the 'sudo' command along with it. For instance, let's say you wish to install the 'jed' text editor. You'll have to type in the following:

'sudo apt-get install jed'

This is how you'll install other packages as well. You'll also want to update the repository whenever you install a brand new package- which is as simple as typing 'sudo apt-get update'. Replace the word 'update' with 'upgrade' to upgrade the distro. Moreover, the 'apt-cache search' command searches for a package.

```
nayso@Alok-Aspire:~$ sudo apt-get install jed
Reading package lists... Done
Building dependency tree
Reading state information... Done
The following extra packages will be installed:
  jed-common libslang2-modules slsh
Suggested packages:
  gpm
The following NEW packages will be installed:
  jed jed-common libslang2-modules slsh
0 upgraded, 4 newly installed, 0 to remove and 419 not upgraded.
Need to get 810 kB of archives.
After this operation, 2,992 kB of additional disk space will be used.
Do you want to continue? [Y/n] █
```

Chmod

When you want to make your file more executable and change the permissions it is granted by Linux, 'chmod' is your command. You can imagine having a python code called 'numbers.py' on your computer. You'll have to run 'python numbers.py' each time you have to run it. Instead of doing that, you can simply run the file by running 'numbers.py' in the terminal. The command 'chmod +x numbers.py' will help you make the file executable in this case. You can give it root permissions with 'chmod 755 numbers.py' or, for root executable, sudo chmod +x numbers.py'.

```
nayso@Alok-Aspire:~/Desktop$ ls
numbers.py
nayso@Alok-Aspire:~/Desktop$ chmod +x numbers.py
nayso@Alok-Aspire:~/Desktop$ ls
numbers.py
```

Hostname

If you want to know the name in your network or host, simply use 'hostname'. It essentially displays your IP address and hostname. If you want to get your network IP address, simply type in 'hostname -i'.

```
nayso@Alok-Aspire:~/Desktop$ hostname
Alok-Aspire
nayso@Alok-Aspire:~/Desktop$ hostname -I
192.168.1.36
```

Ping

This command is great when it comes to checking your connection to a server. For those who are more technically inclined, it is a software utility in computer network administration that you use to test host reachability on an IP network.

Let's take a simple example: when you enter something like 'ping google.com', it checks whether it can connect to the server and come back. This round-trip time is measured and you get the full details about it. People like us however use this command for simple stuff like checking the internet connection.

In our case, if it pings the server (Google), it means your internet connection is active.

```
nayso@Alok-Aspire:~/Desktop$ ping google.com
PING google.com (172.217.26.206) 56(84) bytes of data.
64 bytes from google.com (172.217.26.206): icmp_seq=1 ttl=56 time=51.2 ms
64 bytes from google.com (172.217.26.206): icmp_seq=2 ttl=56 time=47.9 ms
64 bytes from google.com (172.217.26.206): icmp_seq=3 ttl=56 time=48.9 ms
^C
--- google.com ping statistics ---
3 packets transmitted, 3 received, 0% packet loss, time 2000ms
rtt min/avg/max/mdev = 47.959/49.388/51.299/1.417 ms
```

That said, let's create some basic shell scripts using the command line.

How To Create Basic Scripts

When you begin learning the command line interface, you generally explore it interactively. That means that you enter one command at a time so that you see the results of each one.

Take a look at this gif (http://bit.ly/2linux3) which explores a Shakespearean plays' directory using the command line; it counts the number of words and the frequency or how many times the term 'murder' appears in all the plays of Shakespeare.

It's totally fine to use the command-line interface in this interactive manner when you're trying out things but as you may likely notice, typing is one of those activities that are prone to errors. For tasks that are more complex i.e. tasks that you want to repeat, you don't want to retype the code right from the beginning, but make a self-contained shell script that's possible to run as a one-liner.

Your First Shell Script

We'll begin with something simple. Create a junk directory somewhere, like /tmp/my-playground. Your actual workspace doesn't have to be littered with test code.

A shell script is simply a text file that has to make sense. To create one, we'll use the nano text editor.

Nano?

Nano is a text editor. It comes preinstalled in nearly all Linux distros. New users prefer it mainly because of its simplicity, which stands out when compared to other command line text editors like emacs and vi/vim. It basically contains many other useful features like line numbering, syntax coloring and easy search (among others).

Let's continue.

We'll create a shell script called hello.sh. Just follow the following steps:

Type 'nano hello.sh' and run

Nano will open and give you a blank file to work in. Now enter the following shell command.

Echo 'hello world'

On your keyboard, press ctrl +x to exit the editor. When asked whether you want to save the file, press yes (y).

Nano will then confirm whether you want to save the file. Press enter to confirm the action.

Now run the script 'hello. sh' with the following command:

Bash hello.sh

When you look at it as a gif, the steps look something like this.

http://bit.ly/2piclinux

Therefore, 'hello.sh' is not particularly exciting, but at least it catches the essence of what you want to do, which is to wrap up a series of commands into a file, that is, a script, so that you can re-run the script as much as you'd want. That helps you remove the chance of having typographic errors that come about when you're retyping commands, and also allows you to make the script reusable in various contexts.

Having Arguments In A Re-Usable Shell Script

Let's now try making 'hello. sh' a bit complicated. Now instead of repeating hello world, you'll create the script in such a way that it says 'hello' to a certain value- for instance, a person's name. That will make the script seem a bit better. You can use it like so:

```
bash hello.sh Dan

HELLO DAN
```

The gif is as <u>follows</u>.

<u>http://bit.ly/2linux5</u>

First off, you customize 'hello world' by adding a variable in the place of 'world'. Try to do that from the command line interactively:

```
yourname=Dan

echo "Hello $yourname"
```

43

The output is:

Hello Dan

Therefore, the question here is, how do you get the script 'hello.sh' to read in our argument (which is a person's name in this case) that you pass into it?

```
bash hello.sh George
```

You do that through a special bash variable. The first, second and third arguments you passed from the command line into the script are denoted by the variables which include $1, $2, $3. In the example above therefore, the name George will be kept in the variable $1 as 'hello.sh' starts running.

Just reopen 'hello.sh' and change your code to the following

```
$yourname=$1

echo "Hello $yourname"
```

After saving the changes, now run the following to see the output.

```
bash hello.sh Mary
```

If you desire to have the output returned in all caps, simply modify 'hello.sh' in the following manner, making sure to pipe the output through 'tr' in order to replace all the lowercase letters with those in the uppercase.

```
$yourname=$1

echo "Hello $yourname" | tr '[[:lower:]]' '[[:upper:]]'
```

Now if you have a desire to be concise, you may find that '$yourname' variable is not really necessary. The code will be simplified like so:

```
echo "Hello $1" | tr '[[:lower:]]' '[[:upper:]]'
```

Now slow down my friend. If you are able to create a script, you can execute like so:

bash hello.sh

...then congratulations, you've learned an important concept. You've just learned how programmers stuff complicated things into a 'container' that can be run into one line.

It's now time you learnt how to make decisions in your scripts. Keep reading.

Bash "If Statements"

You'll now learn how to automate tasks in your bash scripts using bash if statements. "If statements" essentially allow you to decide whether you should run a piece of code (or not) based on conditions that you may set.

Basic "If Statements"

According to a basic if statement, if a certain test is true, you should then do a certain set of actions. If it is not true, you should not. It follows this format:

```
if [ <some test> ]
then
<commands>
fi
```

Anything that between then and the 'if backwards' denoted by 'fi' is automatically executed if the test (which is between the square brackets) is true. Take a look at this example:

1. #!/bin/bash
2. # Basic if statement
3.
4. if [$1 -gt 100]
5. then
6. echo Hey that\'s a large number.
7. pwd
8. fi
9.
10. date

Just to break it down for you-

We're trying to see whether the first command line argument is more than 100 (in line 4).

In the sixth and seventh line, you can see that it will only run if the test (on the fourth line) returns true. Note you can have whatever number of commands here as you want.

In the sixth line, you can see the backslash before the single quote is required. The single quote has a special meaning for bash and we don't need that special meaning. With the backslash, you are able to escape the special meaning to take it back to a plain single quote.

fi (in the eighth line) marks the end of the if statements. Any command after this will run as normal.

Since this command (in line 10) is outside the if statement, it will run regardless of the if statement's outcome

1. ./if_example.sh 15
2. Mon 14 Jan 0:26:25 2019
3. ./if_example.sh 150
4. Hey that's a large number.
5. /home/ryan/bin
6. Mon 14 Jan 0:26:25 2019
7.

It's always important to test scripts with input that can cover the different possible scenarios.

The Test

These square brackets '[]' that you can see in the 'if' statements reference the 'test' command. That means that all the operators that test allows can be used here too. You can look at some of the most common possible operators below:

Operator	Description
! EXPRESSION	The EXPRESSION is false.
-n STRING	The length of STRING is greater than zero.
-z STRING	The lengh of STRING is zero (ie it is empty).
STRING1 = STRING2	STRING1 is equal to STRING2
STRING1 != STRING2	STRING1 is not equal to STRING2
INTEGER1 -eq INTEGER2	INTEGER1 is numerically equal to INTEGER2
INTEGER1 -gt INTEGER2	INTEGER1 is numerically greater than INTEGER2
INTEGER1 -lt INTEGER2	INTEGER1 is numerically less than INTEGER2
-d FILE	FILE exists and is a directory.
-e FILE	FILE exists.
-r FILE	FILE exists and the read permission is granted.
-s FILE	FILE exists and it's size is greater than zero (ie. it is not empty).
-w FILE	FILE exists and the write permission is granted.
-x FILE	FILE exists and the execute permission is granted.

There are a few things you need to note though:

The sign '=' is a bit different from −eq. Therefore [001 = 1] returns false the same way '=' does a string comparison, and −eq does numerical comparisons which means [001-eq 1] returns true.

The 'file' above refers to a path. A path may refer to a directory or file.

Since [] is simply a reference to the 'test' command, you may experiment then trouble shoot on the command line with test to ensure your understanding of its behavior is right.

1. test 001 = 1
2. echo $?
3. 1
4. test 001 -eq 1
5. echo $?
6. 0
7. touch myfile
8. test -s myfile
9. echo $?
10. 1
11. ls /etc > myfile
12. test -s myfile
13. echo $?
14. 0
15.

Let me break that down a bit for you.

Line 1: do a comparison based comparison. Given that test doesn't print the result, you instead have to check its exit status; that is in the line that follows.

Line 2: the '\$' variable holds the exit status of the command that was previously run (that is, the test). Zero denotes true or success whereas 1 denotes false or failure.

Line 4: you're now doing a numerical comparison

Line 7: a new blank file known as 'myfile' is created- this is assuming that it doesn't exist already.

Line 8: is 'myfile' greater than zero in terms of size?

Line 11: pass on some content into 'myfile' to have its size more than zero.

Line 12: retest the size of the file. It's true this time round.

Final Word: Indenting

Indenting is the manner in which you *organize* and document source code.

As you may notice, we indented the commands (in the 'if' statements above) that run when the statement was true. This is known as indenting and is important when it comes to writing clean code. Indenting helps improve your code's readability and minimizes the chances of making silly mistakes.

It's important to note that there are no indentation rules in bash, which means that you may (or may not indent) and your scripts will run the exact same way.

Nonetheless, particularly as your scripts become bigger, you will find it more difficult to see your scripts' structure, which makes it critical to always have your code indented.

So far, you've learnt more than enough when it comes to using the Linux command line as a beginner. This topic is not complete yet, but the hardest part is. Your job now is to introduce yourself to the following subtopics before you brag about your bash skills:

- Nested if statements

- If else

- If elif else

- Boolean operators and

- Case statements

Conclusion

This book was meant to introduce you to Linux and the Linux command line right from scratch, teach you what you need to know to use it properly and a bit more to take you to the next level. At this point, I can say that you are on your way to doing something great with bash, so don't hang your boots just yet.

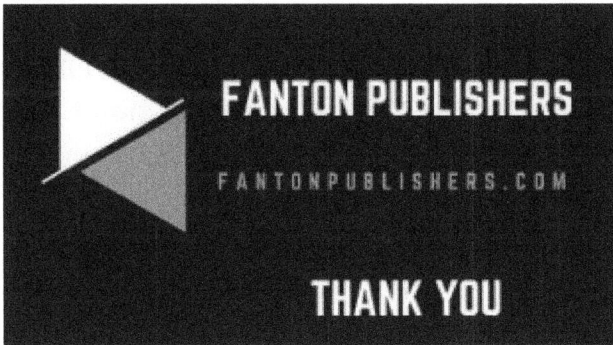

Do You Like My Book & Approach To Publishing?

If you like my writing and style and would love the ease of learning literally everything you can get your hands on from Fantonpublishers.com, I'd really need you to do me either of the following favors.

6 Things

I'll be honest; publishing books on what I learn in my line of work gives me satisfaction. But the biggest satisfaction that I can get as an author is knowing that I am influencing people's lives positively through the content I publish. Greater joy even comes from knowing that customers appreciate the great content that they have read in every book through giving feedback, subscribing to my newsletter, sending emails to tell me how transformative the content they read is, following me on social media and buying several of my books. That's why I am always seeking to engage my readers at a personal level to know them and for them to know me, not just as an author but as a person because we all want to belong. That's why I strive to use different channels to engage my readers so that I can ultimately build a cordial relationship with them for our mutual success i.e. I succeed as an author while at the same time my readers learn stuff that takes days and sometimes weeks to write, edit, format and publish in a matter of hours.

To build this relationship, I'd really appreciate if you could do any or all the following:

1: First, I'd Love It If You Leave a Review of This Book on Amazon.

Let me be honest; reviews play a monumental role in determining whether customers purchase different products online. From the thousands of other books that are on Amazon about the topic, you chose to read this one. I am grateful for that. I may not know why you read my book, especially until the end considering the fact that most readers don't read until the end. Perhaps you purchased this book after reading some of the reviews and were glued with reading the book because it was educative and engaging. Even if you didn't read it because of the positive reviews, perhaps you can make the next customer's purchasing decision a lot easier by posting a review of this book on Amazon!

I'd love it if you did that, as this would help me spread word out about my books and publishing business. The more the readers, the bigger a community we build and we all benefit! If you could leave your honest review of this book on Amazon, I'd be forever grateful (well, I am already grateful to you for purchasing the book and reading it until the end- I don't' take that for granted!). Please Leave a Review of This Book on Amazon.

2: <u>Check Out My Other Books</u>

As I stated earlier, my biggest joy in all this is building an audience that loves my approach to publishing and the amazing content I publish. I know every author has his/her style. Mine is publishing what I learn to readers out there so that they can learn what is trending, what other readers are also searching for in the nonfiction world and much more. As such, if you read the other books I have published, you will undoubtedly know a lot more than the average person on a diverse range of issues. And as you well know, knowledge is power- and the biggest investment that you can ever have on your life!

3: Let's Get In Touch

Let's get closer than just leaving reviews and buying my other books. Reach out to me through email, like or follow me on social media and let's interact. You will perhaps get to know stuff about me that will change your life in a way. As we interact, we will also influence each other in a way. I' definitely would love to learn something from you as we get to know each other.

Antony

Website: http://www.fantonpublishers.com/

Email: Support@fantonpublishers.com

Twitter: https://twitter.com/FantonPublisher

Facebook   Page: https://www.facebook.com/Fantonpublisher/

My   Ketogenic   Diet   Books   Page: **https://www.facebook.com/pg/Fast-Keto-Meals-336338180266944**

Private Facebook Group For Readers: https://www.facebook.com/groups/FantonPublishers/

Pinterest: https://www.pinterest.com/fantonpublisher/

4: Grab Some Freebies On Your Way Out; Giving Is Receiving, Right?

I gave you 2 freebies at the start of the book, one on general life transformation and one about the Ketogenic diet. You are free to choose either or both!

<u>Ketogenic Diet Freebie</u>: http://bit.ly/2fantonpubketo

<u>5 Pillar Life Transformation Checklist</u>: http://bit.ly/2fantonfreebie

5: Suggest Topics That You'd Love Me To Cover To Increase Your Knowledge Bank. As I stated, I love feedback; any type of feedback- positive or negative. As such, make sure to reach out. I am looking forward to seeing your suggestions and insights on the topic. You could even suggest improvements to this book. Simply send me a message on <u>Support@fantonpublishers.com</u>. As a publisher, I strive to publish content that my readers are actively looking for. Therefore, your input is highly important.

6: <u>Subscribe To My Newsletter</u> To Know When I Publish New Books.

I already mentioned this earlier; I love to connect with my readers. This is just another avenue for me to connect to you.

As such, if you would love to know whenever I publish new books and blog posts, subscribe to my newsletter at http://bit.ly/2fantonpubnewbooks. You will be the first to know whenever I have fresh content!

My Other Books

As I already mentioned, I write books on all manner of topics. In this part of the book, I have categorized them all for easy reading. If you wish to receive notifications about a certain category of books, I have provided a link below every category to ensure you only receive what you are looking for.

Weight Loss Books

You can search for the titles on Amazon.

General Weight Loss Books

The books in this category will help you lose weight irrespective of the approach you are using i.e. dieting or workout. I recommend you have them even if you are on specific diets or using specific workouts for weight loss.

Binge Eating: Binge Eating Disorder Cure: Easy To Follow Tips For Eating Only What Your Body Needs

Lose Weight: Lose Weight Fast Naturally: How to Lose Weight Fast Without Having To Become a Gym Rat or Dieting Like a Maniac

Lose Weight: Lose Weight Permanently: Effective Strategies on How to Lose Weight Easily and Permanently

Get updates when we publish any book about weight loss: http://bit.ly/2fantonweightlossbooks

Weight Loss Books On Specific Diets

Ketogenic Diet Books

KETOGENIC DIET: Keto Diet Made Easy: Beginners Guide on How to Burn Fat Fast With the Keto Diet (Including 100+ Recipes That You Can Prepare Within 20 Minutes)- New Edition

KETOGENIC DIET: Ketogenic Diet Recipes That You Can Prepare Using 7 Ingredients and Less in Less Than 30 Minutes

Ketogenic Diet: With A Sustainable Twist: Lose Weight Rapidly With Ketogenic Diet Recipes You Can Make Within 25 Minutes

Ketogenic Diet: Keto Diet Breakfast Recipes

Fat Bombs: Keto Fat Bombs: 50+ Savory and Sweet Ketogenic Diet Fat Bombs That You MUST Prepare Before Any Other!

Snacks: Keto Diet Snacks: 50+ Savory and Sweet Ketogenic Diet Snacks That You MUST Prepare Before Any Other!

Desserts: Keto Diet Desserts: 50+ Savory and Sweet Ketogenic Diet Desserts That You MUST Prepare Before Any Other!

Ketogenic Diet: Ketogenic Diet Lunch and Dinner Recipes

[Ketogenic Diet: Keto Diet Cookbook For Vegetarians](#)

Get updates when we publish any book on the Ketogenic diet: http://bit.ly/2fantonpubketo

Intermittent Fasting Books

[Intermittent Fasting: A Complete Beginners Guide to Intermittent Fasting For Weight Loss, Increased Energy, and A Healthy Life](#)

Get updates when we publish any book on intermittent fasting: http://bit.ly/2fantonbooksIF

Any Other Diet

Get updates when we publish any book on any other diet that will help you to lose weight and keep it off: http://bit.ly/2fantonsdietbooks

Relationships Books

[Wedding: Budget Wedding: Wedding Planning On The Cheap (Master How To Plan A Dream Wedding On Budget)](#)

[How To Get Your Ex Back: Step By Step Formula On How To Get Your Ex Back And Keep Him/her For Good](#)

[SEX POSITIONS: Sex: Unleash The Tiger In You Using These 90-Day Sex Positions With Pictures](#)

Money Problems: How To Solve Relationship Money Problems: Save Your Marriage By Learning How To Fix All Your Money Problems And Save Your Relationship

Family Communication: A Simple Powerful Communication Strategy to Transform Your Relationship with Your Kids and Enjoy Being a Parent Again

Get updates when we publish any book that will help you improve on your personal and professional relationships: http://bit.ly/2fantonsrelations

Personal Development

Body Language: Master Body Language: A Practical Guide to Understanding Nonverbal Communication and Improving Your Relationships

Subconscious Mind: Tame, Reprogram & Control Your Subconscious Mind To Transform Your Life

Emotional Intelligence: The Mindfulness Guide To Mastering Your Emotions, Getting Ahead And Improving Your Life

Habits: The Habit Blueprint: 15 Simple Steps to Transform Your Life and Create Lasting Change without Feeling Overwhelmed and Frustrated

Get updates when we publish any book that will help you become a better person by boosting your

productivity, achieving more of your goals, beating procrastination, breaking bad habits, forming new habits, beat stress, building your self-esteem and confidence and much more: http://bit.ly/2fantonpubpersonaldevl

Personal Finance & Investing Books

Real Estate: Rental Property Investment Guide: How To Buy & Manage Rental Property For Profits

MONEY: Make Money Online: 150+ Real Ways to Make Real Money Online (Plus 50 Bonus Tips to Guarantee Your Success)

Money: How To Make Money Online: Make Money Online In 101 Ways

Get updates when we publish any book that will help you up your game in personal finance and investing: http://bit.ly/2fantonpersfinbooks

Health & Fitness Books

PMS CURE: Easy To Follow Home Remedies For PMS & PMDD

Testosterone: How to Boost Your Testosterone Levels in 15 Different Ways Naturally

Hair Loss: How to Stop Hair Loss: Actionable Steps to Stop Hair Loss (Hair Loss Cure, Hair Care, Natural Hair Loss Cures)

Hashimoto's: Hashimoto's Cookbook: Eliminate Toxins and Restore Thyroid Health through Diet In 1 Month

Stress: The Psychology of Managing Pressure: Practical Strategies to turn Pressure into Positive Energy (5 Key Stress Techniques for Stress, Anxiety, and Depression Relief)

Hormone Reset Diet: Over 30 Hormone Reset Diet Recipes to Balanced Hormone, FAST Weight Loss, Lower Stress, Better Immune System, and Faster Metabolism

Get updates when we publish any book that will help you up your game in health and fitness: http://bit.ly/2fantonhealthnfit

Book Summaries

This category will feature summaries of some of your favorite books, written in a manner you can easily digest and follow:

Summary: The Millionaire Next Door: The Surprising Secrets of America's Wealthy

Summary: The Plant Paradox: The Hidden Dangers In "Healthy" Foods That Cause Disease And Weight Gain

Get updates whenever we publish new book summaries: http://bit.ly/2fantons

All The Other Niches

This category of books includes anything that we cannot realistically fit in the categories above. As always, if you want just about anything you can get to read, this is the category for you!

Travel Books

Kenya: Travel Guide: The Traveler's Guide to Make The Most Out of Your Trip to Kenya (Kenya Tourists Guide)

Dog Training

<u>Dog Tricks: 15 Tricks You Must Teach Your Dog before Anything Else</u>

World Issues Books

<u>ISIS/ISIL: The Rise and Rise of the Islamic State: A Comprehensive Guide on ISIS & ISIL</u>

Get notifications when we publish books on anything else above from the niches I mentioned above: http://bit.ly/2fantonpubnewbooks

See You On The Other Side!

See, I publish books on just about any topic imaginable!

If you have any suggestions on topics you would want me to cover, feel free to get in touch:

Website: http://www.fantonpublishers.com/

Email: Support@fantonpublishers.com

Twitter: https://twitter.com/FantonPublisher

My Ketogenic Diet Books Page: https://www.facebook.com/pg/Fast-Keto-Meals-336338180266944

Facebook Page: https://www.facebook.com/Fantonpublisher/

Private Facebook Group For Readers: https://www.facebook.com/groups/FantonPublishers/

Pinterest: https://www.pinterest.com/fantonpublisher/

PS: You can subscribe to my mailing list to know when I publish new books:

Hey! This is not the entire list! You can check an updated list of all my books on:

My Author Central: amazon.com/author/fantonpublishers

My Website: http://www.fantonpublishers.com

Stay With Me On My Journey To Making Passive Income Online

I have to admit; my writing business makes several six figures a year in profits (after paying ourselves salaries). Until recently, I didn't realize just how hard we worked to build this business to what it has become so far.

However, while it is profitable and I want to do it in the long term, I understand its limitations. I know I cannot have an endless number of writers at a time especially if we are to continue delivering high quality products to our customers and readers consistently.

That's why I have recently started getting more serious with self-publishing to help me build a passive income business i.e. income that is not pegged on the number of writers and hours that we put to develop our products.

Thanks to my vast experience and dedication to get things done, I am committed to building a six figure passive income publishing business.

To make sure you are part of this journey, I am inviting you to subscribe to our newsletter (http://bit.ly/2fanton6figprogress) to know my progress as far as passive income generation is concerned. That's not all; if making passive income, just like me, is something you'd love to venture into, you can follow my 'tell it all' blog, which I explain everything I have done to promote every book and how the results are turning out with figures and images.

My goal is to make sure that while I add value to my audience through the different topics that I publish about to solve various problems for instance, I also add massive value to readers in ways that go beyond just one book. Subscribe to our newsletter to know when I publish new books, how I did market research, how I make money with the books and much, much more.

You can even ask questions on anything you want me to answer regarding publishing and everything else related to the topics of discussion.

Antony

Website: http://www.fantonpublishers.com/

Email: Support@fantonpublishers.com

Twitter: https://twitter.com/FantonPublisher

Facebook   Page: https://www.facebook.com/Fantonpublisher/

My   Ketogenic   Diet   Books   Page: https://www.facebook.com/pg/Fast-Keto-Meals-336338180266944

Private   Facebook   Group   For   Readers: https://www.facebook.com/groups/FantonPublishers/

Pinterest: https://www.pinterest.com/fantonpublisher/

I look forward to hearing from you!

PSS: Let Me Also Help You Save Some Money!

If you are a heavy reader, have you considered subscribing to Kindle Unlimited? You can read this and millions of other books for just $9.99 a month)! You can check it out by searching for Kindle Unlimited on Amazon!

www.ingramcontent.com/pod-product-compliance
Lightning Source LLC
Chambersburg PA
CBHW031909200326
41597CB00012B/564